HOLY TRADITION

Ecclesial Experience of Life in Christ

HOLY TRADITION

Ecclesial Experience of Life in Christ

HARRY BOOSALIS

ST. TIKHON'S MONASTERY PRESS
SOUTH CANAAN, PENNSYLVANIA
2013

HOLY TRADITION
Ecclesial Experience of Life in Christ

The icon of Pentecost on the front cover
is a detail from the 16th century by Theophan the Cretan
used with the kind permission of
Stavronikita Monastery, Mount Athos

Cover design by Kenyon Theophan Mackey.

Published by:
St. Tikhon's Monastery Press
175 St. Tikhon's Road
Waymart, Pennsylvania 18472
USA

Printed in the United States of America

ISBN 978-0-9884574-2-3

Dedicated to

Father Anthony M. Coniaris

my spiritual father in Christ

TABLE OF CONTENTS

ABOUT THE AUTHOR

Dr. Harry M. Boosalis, Th. D., a native of Minneapolis, received his Bachelor of Arts degree in Philosophy and Classics from the University of Minnesota. Graduating from Holy Cross Greek Orthodox School of Theology (Master of Divinity degree, Class of 1985) he went on to receive his doctoral degree in Orthodox Theology from the University of Thessaloniki under the direction of Professor Georgios Mantzaridis. He is Professor of Dogmatic Theology at St. Tikhon's Orthodox Seminary where he has been teaching since the Fall of 1992. His other books include *Taught by God*, *Knowledge of God*, *Orthodox Spiritual Life* and *The Joy of the Holy*, also published by St. Tikhon's Press.

PREFACE

This study focuses on the vital role of Holy Tradition within the life of the Orthodox Church. Special attention is given to how Holy Tradition serves as the common font of the shared spiritual and liturgical life, as well as the theological teachings that unite all Orthodox as one.

Topics such as 'Christ as the Core of Holy Tradition', 'Tradition as the Life of the Holy Spirit within the Church', 'Oral Tradition and Written Tradition', 'Tradition as Personal Participation', and the proper relationship between Tradition and ethnic customs are discussed.

Based on Holy Scripture and patristic teaching, this study refers to the writings of a wide variety of Orthodox theologians, especially those of Eastern European backgrounds.

Although intended as introductory lectures for first-year seminarians, the reader-friendly style of *HOLY TRADITION: Ecclesial Experience of Life in Christ* is ideal for anyone interested in Eastern Christian spirituality and the study of Orthodox theology.

All Scriptural quotations are taken from the
New King James Version, unless otherwise noted.

Therefore, brethren, stand fast and hold the traditions which you were taught, whether by word or our epistle.

The Apostle Paul
(First Century)

Concerning the teachings of the Church ... we have received some from written sources, while others have been given to us secretly, through apostolic tradition. Both sources have equal force ...

St. Basil the Great
(Fourth Century)

We will not remove the age-old landmarks which our fathers have set, but we keep the tradition we have received. For if we begin to erode the foundations of the Church even a little, in no time at all the whole edifice will fall to the ground.

St. John Damascene
(Eighth Century)

Holy Tradition

Ecclesial Experience of Life in Christ

Prologue: Holy Tradition Today

Upon arriving at our seminary, a first year student once asked me how I felt about all the differences that exist among the various ethnic traditions of the Orthodox Church. Doesn't the disparity of expressions point to an inconsistency in the oneness of our Faith? Isn't it obvious how different we all are, in terms of the variety of our liturgical languages, Church music, iconography and architecture—even the local saints who are venerated in one jurisdiction but not necessarily in others? How are we supposed to explain this apparent divergence, where all the distinctive national jurisdictions have their own local traditions which seem to separate themselves from one another? Don't such discrepancies detract from the unity of our supposedly One, Holy, Catholic and Apostolic Faith?

Actually, I assured him, the exact opposite is true.

While it is not unusual to highlight the diversity that definitely exists within our different jurisdictions, there is at the same time an extraordinary unity and harmony of life which is also apparent within the various ethnic expressions of Holy Tradition. These include our shared sacramental life and liturgical services, our identical spiritual life and theological doctrines, as well as our common moral and canonical teachings, to name a few.

This shared experience of Holy Tradition is truly remarkable for its unanimity and unique continuity that stretches throughout the long history of the Orthodox Church. Rather than focusing on the minute details of diversity—which in fact enrich and enliven our singular Orthodox Faith—more attention should be given to the organic wholeness of our living Tradition. It is this organic wholeness which indeed unites all Orthodox believers through our shared ecclesial life in Christ.

By sharing in this same ecclesial life of the Orthodox Church, following the same liturgical cycles, singing the same hymns, reciting the same prayers and following the same ways of prayer, being inspired by the same Scriptural readings, observing the same fasts and celebrating the same feasts—all Orthodox believers, from throughout the centuries of the Church's existence, share a common Faith and communal experience of the abundant life in Christ. In this unique way, all Orthodox Christians are united as one in the timeless and eternal bond of two thousand years of Holy Tradition.

Every culture which embraces the Orthodox Faith makes its own unique contribution to the Church's manifold expression of her life in Christ. This is how a simple Russian monk near Moscow can cross the Bering Strait and bring this Holy Tradition to the New World. This is how Holy Tradition becomes incarnate within the culture of the native Indians of the Aleutian Islands. This is how the veneration of St. Herman of Alaska, the great 'North Star of Christ's Holy Church', shines forth from the Arctic Circle and enlightens all of America, Europe and beyond, embracing even Mount Athos itself.

Yes, there are certain local or ethnic customs not shared by all, and even certain saints whose veneration may not be quite so widespread. Yet this diversity in itself does not detract from our ecclesial unity. It in fact bears witness to the inherent freedom of the dynamic life of our One, Holy, Catholic and Apostolic Church.

This present study focuses on the vital role of Holy Tradition within the life of the Orthodox Church. Special attention is given to how Holy Tradition serves as the common font of our shared spiritual and liturgical life as well as the theological teachings that unite all Orthodox as one.

Topics such as 'The Life in Christ as the Core of Holy Tradition', 'Tradition as the Life of the Holy Spirit within the Church', and the inherent interdependence between 'Holy Tradition and Holy Scripture' are addressed, as are 'Tradition as Personal Participation', 'Tradition and Catholic Consciousness', and the fundamental role of Orthodox monasticism within the life of Holy Tradition. Finally, the proper relationship between ethnic customs and Holy Tradition will also be discussed. Special emphasis is given to the Orthodox Churches in the so called 'diaspora', including North America, Western Europe and Australia.

Orthodox Churches in these countries find themselves in a rather peculiar position. On the one hand, they have been established within the traditions of particular Orthodox cultures from their perspective 'mother countries'. Yet on the other hand, as these first generations pass, and as their Churches continually grow and thrive, new generations of Orthodox believers are coming to identify more with the culture of their now 'native' countries.

Orthodox Churches of the 'diaspora' (if indeed that word is even still applicable) are now faced with questions concerning the degree to which they should allow themselves to embrace the natural assimilation within the national culture of their home countries.

To add to the novelty of this situation is the increasing number of converts to the Orthodox Faith. In many cases, these new Orthodox believers have had little or no exposure to the life of Holy Tradition, in any form or ethnic culture. Both the hierarchy and the faithful of these Churches must not only navigate between the various ethnic traditions of the established national jurisdictions, but they must also determine whether or not—and to what degree—they are to forge and embrace their own Orthodox identity within the native culture of their own country.

I recall from my own student years at the University of Thessaloniki, how a close friend and fellow classmate from Indonesia once asked an elder from Mount Athos how he was supposed to establish the Orthodox

Church in his native country. "Geronda," he asked, "how am I supposed to help my fellow Indonesians become Orthodox? How will they learn to *feel* Orthodox and come to *think* like Orthodox Christians? Do they first have to become Greek? Do they first have to speak Greek and worship in Greek? Is that the goal of my mission in Indonesia?"

"No," replied the Elder emphatically. "They will become Orthodox, not when they become Greek, but when they become truly Indonesian."

Introductory Remarks

The Orthodox Church does not exist apart from Holy Tradition. Holy Tradition is the very source from which the life-giving waters of Orthodox spiritual life and theology pour forth. Holy Tradition constitutes both the means and the manifestation of the Church's mystical participation in the life in Christ. Through Holy Tradition the Body and Blood of Christ remain mystically present in His Church.

The Divine Eucharist holds a preeminent place within the life of Holy Tradition.[1] The Divine Eucharist is the means by which Christ's deified and deifying Blood is transfused into the believer's very own veins. St. Nicholas Cabasilas teaches clearly, "Christ infuses Himself into us and mingles Himself with us. He changes and transforms us into Himself; as a small drop of water is changed by being poured into an immense sea of ointment ... we are mingled with Him in soul and united to Him in body and commingled in blood. ... He pours His Blood into the hearts of those who have been initiated."[2]

---

[1] Cf. G. Mantzaridis, *Time and Man*, South Canaan, 1996, p. 62.

[2] St. Nicholas Cabasilas, *The Life in Christ* 4. 6, 10 and 17, trans. C. deCatanzaro, Crestwood, 1974, pp. 123, 129 and 141. He writes elsewhere, "While natural food is changed into him who feeds on it, and fish and bread and any other kind of food become human blood, here it is entirely opposite. The Bread of Life Himself changes him who feeds on Him and transforms and assimilates him into Himself." Ibid. 4. 8, p. 126. See also *The Prayers of Thanksgiving After Holy Communion*, A Prayer of St. Simeon

In this light, it is not only our participation in the Holy Eucharist, but our participation in the life of Holy Tradition as a whole which also serves as the conduit whereby the vivifying and deifying life in Christ is infused into the members of His Body.

Attempts at a Definition

As is well known, the Greek word for 'tradition' is παράδοσις, which implies a 'handing over', 'transmission' or 'handing down'.[3] Its verbal form is παραδίδωμι.[4] In Latin the noun *traditio*, (or *trado* in its verbal form), has similar meaning.[5] As used in the New Testament and patristic writings, the words παράδοσις and παραδίδωμι, together with their variant verbal forms, may also refer to that which is 'delivered'.[6] Another closely associated term is παραλαμβάνω, which means 'to take, take over, receive or accept'.[7]

Metaphrastes, "Consume me not, O My Creator, but instead enter into my members, my veins, my heart ..." South Canaan, 1984, p. 187.

[3] See *A Patristic Greek Lexicon*, ed. G. Lampe, Oxford, 1982, p. 1014.

[4] See ibid., p. 1013.

[5] See *A Latin Dictionary*, ed. C. Lewis and C. Short, Oxford, 1888, pp. 1883-1884.

[6] See *A Greek-English Lexicon of the New Testament*, ed. Bauer, Chicago, 1979, p. 614 and *A Patristic Greek Lexicon*, p. 1014.

[7] See *A Greek-English Lexicon of the New Testament*, p. 619.

For the Apostle Paul, the content of this Tradition which is 'received', 'given over', 'delivered' or 'accepted' is none other than the life in the crucified and risen Christ.

For example, he writes to the Corinthians, "For I delivered [παρέδωκα] to you first of all that which I also received [παρέλαβον]: that Christ died for our sins according to the Scriptures, and that He was buried, and that He rose again the third day ..."[8]

Furthermore, in the same epistle, he also writes from a specific eucharistic perspective, "For I received [παρέλαβον] from the Lord that which I also delivered [παρέδωκα] to you; that the Lord Jesus on the same night in which He was betrayed took bread; and when He had given thanks, He broke it and said, 'Take, eat; this is My body which is broken for you; do this in remembrance of Me."[9]

For St. Paul it was imperative for the success of his mission that the churches he founded maintain the traditions he was teaching, by passing them on and keeping them whole, intact and unaltered: "Therefore, brethren, stand fast and hold the traditions [παραδόσεις] which you were taught, whether by word or our epistle."[10] And elsewhere, "Now I praise you, brethren, that you remember me in all things and keep the traditions [παραδόσεις] just as I delivered [παρέδωκα] them to you."[11] He also exhorts the Colossians, "As you therefore have received [παρελάβετε] Christ Jesus the

---

[8] 1 Cor. 15. 3, 4.
[9] 1 Cor. 11. 23, 24.
[10] 2 Thess. 2. 15.
[11] 1 Cor. 11. 2.

Lord, so walk in Him. ... Beware lest anyone cheat you through philosophy and empty deceit, according to the tradition [παράδοσιν] of men, according to the basic principles of the world, and not according to Christ."[12] Clearly, the content of the Tradition referred to by the Apostle Paul in the New Testament has the life in Christ at its core.

Nonetheless, it is very difficult to provide a concise and clear-cut definition of Holy Tradition. There is no single, simple description that succinctly captures the breadth and depth of its entire meaning. Vladimir Lossky describes the problematic nature of attempting to define Holy Tradition:

> Tradition is one of those terms which, through being too rich in meanings, runs the risk of finally having none. ... One is reduced to definitions which embrace too many things at a time and which no longer capture what constitutes the real meaning of 'Tradition'. As soon as precision is desired, the over-abundant content has to be broken up and a group of narrow concepts created, the sum of which is far from expressing that living reality called the Tradition of the Church.[13]

When attempting to define Holy Tradition, it is sometimes helpful to mention first what it is *not*. While there is obviously a conservative element within Holy

---

[12] Col. 2. 6, 8. Cf. Gal. 1. 8, 9; 1 Thess. 2. 13.
[13] V. Lossky, *In the Image and Likeness of God*, Crestwood, 1985, p. 141.

Tradition, which entails a firm focus and desire to preserve the purity of the faith, still there are those who at
times misunderstand and misinterpret its true meaning.

For instance, Holy Tradition is not a rigid deter-
mination to simply hold on to what is ancient and anti-
quated; neither is it narrow-minded stubbornness to remain old-fashioned and outdated. Holy Tradition is not
blind conservatism; neither is it a reactionary retreat
from the contemporary world. Holy Tradition is not
emotional attachment to particular ethnic customs; neither is it sentimental devotion to local religious practices of a bygone era.[14]

Holy Tradition must not be seen as something
stagnant. Its intention is not to stifle, but rather to renew
and regenerate life. *Holy* Tradition is a *living* Tradition.
It *gives* true life to those who live it. Its nature is dynamic. It is vibrant and it vivifies all those who actively
pursue it, through their personal participation in the life
of the Church. Professor Georgios Mantzaridis defines
Tradition as "the way of the Church ... the *truth* of the
Church. ... [and] the *life* of the Church."[15] In this more
positive light, other Orthodox theologians also offer
many constructive definitions of Holy Tradition, each
with particular nuances of their own.

As an example, Metropolitan Kallistos (Ware),
speaking of its direct link to the age of the Apostles,
refers to Holy Tradition as "the faith and practice which

---

[14] E.g., J. Meyendorff, *Catholicity and the Church*, Crestwwood,
1983, p. 85; G. Florovsky, *Creation and Redemption*, Belmont,
1976, p. 194; G. Mantzaridis, *Time and Man*, pp. 68-69.
[15] G. Mantzaridis, *Time and Man*, trans. J. Vulliamy, p. 62.

Jesus Christ imparted to the Apostles, and which since the Apostles' time has been handed down from generation to generation in the Church."[16]

Professor Constantine Scouteris also discusses Holy Tradition in terms of its direct correlation with the life of the Church. He writes, "Through Tradition the Church is preserved alive and changeless simply because only in Tradition can the authentic message of Revelation be found, and only through Tradition does the life of the Church arrive at each given moment in time."[17]

Elsewhere he clearly identifies the Church with Holy Tradition itself, "The Church *is* Tradition, and Tradition, in its turn, is understood as the conscience of the Church. Hence, it is impossible for one to speak about Tradition without at the same time speaking about the Church."[18] In a similar way, Lossky relates Holy Tradition to the 'consciousness' of the Church.[19]

---

[16] T. Ware, *The Orthodox Church*, London, 1997, p. 196.

[17] C. Scouteris, 'Paradosis: The Orthodox Understanding of Tradition' in *Ecclesial Being*, ed. C. Veniamin, South Canaan, 2005, p. 133.

[18] Ibid., p. 131 (emphasis mine).

[19] Cf. V. Lossky, *In the Image and Likeness of God*, pp. 154-155.

Holy Tradition and 'Catholic Consciousness'

Our personal participation in the life of Holy Tradition is intimately related to our own self-awareness as members of the Body of Christ. It is also clearly connected to our own 'consciousness' of the catholic fullness of the Orthodox Church. Through Holy Tradition we become cognizant of the fullness of the truth revealed to us through the life of the Church. We are made conscious of our participation in the distinct and dynamic dimensions of ecclesial life which are diversely experienced, yet apprehended as a whole. We become conscious of the innate and organic unity of the life of Holy Tradition, wherein as believing members of the Body of Christ we become bonded, not only to Christ but also to each other.[20]

Commenting on our conscious transformation toward this catholic fullness of the life of the Church, Fr. Florovsky offers the following:

> To know or perceive through Tradition means to know or perceive from the fullness of this experience ... And this can be known within the Church by each person in his personal experience, according to the measure of his spiritual maturity. To turn oneself toward Tradition means to turn oneself toward this fullness.

---

[20] Cf. St. Cyril of Alexandria, *Commentary on the Gospel of John* 11. 1; PG74, 560AD.

The 'Catholic transformation' of consciousness makes it possible for each person to
know—not in fact for himself only but for
all...[21]

In this particular case, the term 'catholic' is used
more in a *qualitative* rather than a *quantitative* context.[22] In addition to its sometimes quantitative sense of
meaning 'universal' which refers to an "external universality", the term 'catholic' can also have a more
qualitative connotation referring to the totality or fullness of the apostolic Faith. The life of Holy Tradition
leads to the full and abundant life—that life where
nothing is lacking—which Christ promises to His disciples, "I came that they may have life, and have it
abundantly."[23] For Fr. Florovsky, "The faithfulness to
Tradition is not a loyalty to antiquity but rather the living relationship with the fullness of the Christian life.
The appeal to Tradition is not so much the appeal to
earlier patterns as it is an appeal to the 'catholic' experience of the Church, to the fullness of her knowledge."[24]

---

[21] G. Florovsky, *Creation and Redemption*, p. 40. Cf. G. Florovsky, *Ways of Russian Theology*, vol. 2, Belmont, 1987, pp. 294-
295.

[22] See Florovsky, "The term 'catholic' is often understood wrong-
ly and imprecisely. [It] does not at all mean an external universality—it is not a quantitative but rather a qualitative criterion." *Creation and Redemption*, p. 37.

[23] John 10. 10.

[24] G. Florovsky, *Creation and Redemption*, p. 37.

Holy Tradition as Personal Participation

The extent to which the believer is able to discern the depths and diverse dimensions of this 'fullness' of the catholic life of Holy Tradition is proportional to his spiritual purity. According to Orthodox teaching, man strives toward his salvation and sanctification as a *co-worker* with God.

The patristic term is *synergy* (συνέργεια), which means 'working with' or the 'co-operation' of man with God.[25] In man's relationship with Christ, divine grace works synergistically with human freedom. In this sense, one's quality of life within the Holy Church and his capacity to perceive and participate in the life of Holy Tradition depends directly on one's willingness to 'work at'[26] and strive for all that the Lord has promised him—indeed to acquire the grace of *the* Promise—through the purification of one's passions, which leads to spiritual illumination and ultimately to sanctification, deification or *theosis* in Christ: "Behold, I send the Promise of My Father upon you; but tarry in the city of Jerusalem until you are endued with power from on high."[27]

---

[25] See *A Patristic Greek Lexicon*, p. 1323.

[26] "Work out your own salvation with fear and trembling." Phil. 2. 12.

[27] Luke 24. 49. Cf. Acts 1. 4. See also the dismissal hymn (*apolytikion*) for the Feast of the Ascension.

The Apostle Peter exhorts the faithful to strive to obtain the fullness of this promise of our rightful inheritance as fellow disciples of Christ, "Grace and peace be multiplied to you in the knowledge of God and of Jesus our Lord, as His divine power has given to us all things that pertain to life and godliness ... by which have been given to us exceedingly great and precious promises, that through these you may be partakers of the divine nature ..."[28] The Apostle Paul also reminds us of the divine inheritance we share together with the Saints, "... giving thanks to the Father who has qualified us to be partakers of the inheritance of the saints in the light."[29]

From an Orthodox perspective, it is only those believers who have been baptized and united to the Body of Christ—who are 'working out' and progressing in the purification of their passions and striving toward illumination and theosis—who are rightly considered as legitimate heirs and authentic bearers and transmitters of the precious inheritance of apostolic Tradition. Only those members of the Church who have been and continue to be purified of the passions, who know God through divine illumination and who are being deified through the divine grace of the Holy Spirit through their participation in the life of the Church—it is only *they* who truly recognize and receive the inheritance of apostolic Tradition and truly participate in it and pass it on.

---

[28] 2 Peter 1. 4.
[29] Col. 1. 12. Cf. Acts 20. 32; Eph. 1. 11.

Along these lines Fr. John Romanides makes an interesting observation. Among those who receive, guard and transmit Holy Tradition, he clearly distinguishes two kinds of believers. The first consists of those who know God through their *direct* experience of His divine grace and glory, namely the deified Prophets, Apostles and Saints of the Church. The second is composed of more simple believers, who humbly *accept* and *embrace* the witness and inspired teachings of those who truly 'know' God.[30]

According to Fr. Romanides, both groups of believers indeed participate in the life of divine grace through the ascetic, liturgical and sacramental life of the Church, yet on different levels. As participants in the glory of Christ, the deified *directly* experience divine revelation which transcends any created means of expression through words, images and symbols. We simple believers, as members of the Holy Church, are also exposed to and participate to a certain degree, in this same grace-filled life of Holy Tradition. Yet for the present, due to our lack of spiritual purification and illumination, it remains hidden among created words, images, symbols, and liturgical ceremonies and sacramental rites.[31]

---

[30] See J. Romanides, *Δογματικὴ καὶ Συμβολικὴ Θεολογία τῆς Ὀρθοδόξου Καθολικῆς Ἐκκλησίας*, vol. 1, Thessaloniki, 2004, p. 124. Cf. J. Romanides, *An Outline of Orthodox Patristic Dogmatics*, ed. and trans. G. Dragas, Rollinsford, 2004, pp. 85-87.

[31] See J. Romanides, *Δογματικὴ καὶ Συμβολικὴ Θεολογία τῆς Ὀρθοδόξου Καθολικῆς Ἐκκλησίας*, vol. 1, p. 129. Cf. J. Romanides, *An Outline of Orthodox Patristic Dogmatics*, p. 87.

However, we too as members of His Holy Body are destined—depending on the degree of our spiritual purity—to experience Christ's uncreated glory in a similar way, just as the Apostles experienced it on Mount Tabor during His Transfiguration and as the Saints experienced it after Pentecost.[32] The Apostle Paul teaches, "But as it is written, 'Eye has not seen, nor ear heard, nor have entered into the heart of man the things which God has prepared for those who love Him'. But God has revealed them to us through His Spirit."[33]

Catechumens, on the other hand, are still on their way; they are *in via*. They have not yet reached their destination. They are still gradually being formed within the womb of the Body of the Church. They may be blessed with spatters and sprinkles of the Truth, but they are not yet fully submerged in the life of Holy Tradition. They do not yet dive into the depths of the divine life of the Church. They have not yet been born through the waters of the baptismal font. They may have a foretaste and savor the flavor of certain *traces* of the Truth, but they do not yet feast at the banquet table of the Lord. They do not yet feed on the deified Flesh and Blood of Christ. Properly speaking, they do not yet participate in the sacramental fullness of the catholic life of the Orthodox Church.

Elder Vasileios of Iveron Monastery on Mount Athos emphasizes the significance of how full participation in the life in Christ requires communion with

---

[32] See J. Romanides, *Δογματικὴ καὶ Συμβολικὴ Θεολογία τῆς Ὀρθοδόξου Καθολικῆς Ἐκκλησίας*, vol. 1, p. 129. Cf. J. Romanides, *An Outline of Orthodox Patristic Dogmatics*, p. 87.
[33] 1 Cor. 2. 9,10.

Him through the fullness of the life of His Body—the Holy Church. There is no room here for partial participation. Our *whole* life is affected and transformed. He compares our personal participation in the catholic fullness of the life of the Church to the sacrament of Holy Baptism:

> The whole body of the Church bears witness to the unifying grace of the Trinity... We cannot leave anything outside the baptism which is of Christ. ... And if you keep one aspect of your life removed from the 'strange and most glorious change', you affect the entire mystery, putting your whole life out of joint... Orthodox baptism, as a triple immersion of the whole body and not just a partial sprinkling, is seen here also to be profoundly symbolic and applicable to the whole of the Church's life.[34]

To experience the fullness of the life in Christ necessarily entails our personal participation in the life of Holy Tradition, whereby we experience the catholic fullness of the life of the Church.[35] Here we begin to appreciate the experiential side of the life of Tradition.

---

[34] Archim. Vasileios, *Hymn of Entry*, trans. E. Briere, Crestwood, 1984, pp. 47-48.

[35] Cf. Fr. Florovsky, "Faithfulness to Tradition is ... the living relationship with the fullness of the Christian life. ... Tradition is known and understood only by belonging to the Church, through participation in her common or 'catholic' life." *Creation and Redemption*, p. 37.

We are not called to simply 'follow' Tradition or 'mimic' Tradition. We are called to experience it within our own daily lives. We must *live* Holy Tradition just as the Saints have done and continue to do. Tradition must come to truly exist within us. And it can only exist within us, whenever we freely choose to follow and embrace it.

As faithful members of the Body of Christ we thus find our true life—again that true and *abundant* life promised by our Lord to His disciples—only within the life of Holy Tradition.[36] And this is contingent on our continued progress in purity and spiritual maturity:

> In the catholic nature of the Church there is the possibility of theological *knowledge* ... each person *can* realize the catholic standard in himself. I do not say that each person *does* realize it. That depends upon the measure of one's spiritual maturity. Each person is, however, called. And those who realize it we call Fathers and Teachers of the Church, for we hear from them not simply their personal opinions but the very *witness* of the Church—because they speak out of the Catholic fullness.[37]

These words are important for all believers today; yet they are more significant for students of Orthodox theology, especially those who are called to become our

---

[36] Cf. John 10. 10.
[37] G. Florovsky, *Creation and Redemption*, p. 40.

parish priests tomorrow. Our priests must never forget
that what they are called to witness to, what they are
expected to preach and teach, and what we want to hear
and see from them, is not in fact their *own* personal
opinions or ideas concerning the various practices and
beliefs of our Church. What we are looking for, and
what we are counting on, is to see some sense of this
'catholic standard' within their own lives—both on a
personal level as well as on a *pastoral* level, as they
serve our families and communities as our local parish
priest.

In fact the only thing they really have to offer
their people comes ultimately from their own personal
experience of the life of Holy Tradition; from their own
life within the Church; from their own practice and progress in prayer. And while we do not expect our parish
priests to be proclaimed as holy elders or canonized as
Orthodox Saints, we *do* expect some sense of ecclesial
integrity with respect to their faithfulness to Holy Tradition.

What is looked for in an Orthodox priest is not so
much a charismatic individual, an educated scholar or a
licensed therapist, which are not necessarily hindrances
to one's ordained ministry. First and foremost, however, what the Church seeks is simply a *man* of the
Church—a bona-fide 'Church man'—someone who obviously *belongs* to the Church; someone who clearly
knows the Church; and someone we can confidently
count on to actually *represent* the Church, especially in
our times of trouble and tragedy, sickness and pain.

In a certain sense the priest personifies or even 'incarnates' the Church, in as much as he represents God to His people and serves them in the image of Christ. This is why we call our priests 'Father'. This is why we kiss their hand. The priest has been ordained and set apart for a unique and holy ministry.

This is most apparent during the celebration of the Divine Liturgy. His sacred vestments clearly set him apart from the ordinary. The cuffs he wears around his wrists reveal the spiritual reality that his human hands are now acting as the hands of God. They are not just his hands alone any longer, but the hands of Christ reaching out and feeding His children. Likewise the voice of the celebrant priest, as it resonates with the message of God speaking to His people, is no longer just his alone, but the voice of Christ proclaiming His Gospel to the world.

And all this is only realized, whether regarding the ministry of the local parish priest or within the life of the lay believer, through the acquisition of this 'consciousness' of the 'catholic fullness' of Holy Tradition, where the fullness of the abundant life in Christ is found.

The fullness of this catholic and apostolic life of the Orthodox Church is offered to the believer through his direct and experiential participation in the life of Holy Tradition. This catholic life of apostolic Tradition, which is lived by faith through the grace of the Holy Spirit, is the same as that experienced by the holy Apostles themselves. It stems from their same sacramental setting of worship. It extends from their same eucharistic experience of communion with Jesus Christ.

It lives through the same liturgical life leading from the Upper Room.

Elder Porphyrios shares his experience of Holy Tradition. He emphasizes the importance of our personal participation in the liturgical life of the Holy Church and how it unites us not only with Christ, but also with each other:

> The divine services are words in which we converse and speak to God with our worship and with our love. The hours spent closest to paradise are the hours spent in the church together with all our brethren when we celebrate the Divine Liturgy, when we sing and when we receive Holy Communion. Together we all follow the divine services—the words of our Lord. With the Gospel, the Epistles, the hymns of the Book of the Eight Tones, of the Lenten Triodion, and of the Offices of the Saints, we achieve our union with Christ.[38]

Indeed liturgical worship lies at the very center of the life of the Orthodox Church.[39] To worship Christ remains the ultimate focus of Holy Tradition.

---

[38] Elder Porphyrios, *Wounded by Love*, trans. J. Raffin, Evia, Greece, 2005, p. 165.

[39] Cf. G. Mantzaridis, "Worship is the center of the Church's life ... If worship is missing, the presence and work of the Church have no meaning, while with worship at the center, the presence and work of the Church, as of each particular member, acquire sense and purpose." *Orthodox Spiritual Life*, trans. K. Schram, Brookline, 1994, p. 70.

All the sacramental rites and rituals, and all the prayers and various forms of liturgical practice that make up the life of Holy Tradition, are all centered on the worship of Christ.[40] It is the Person of Christ, and the divine life of the Holy Trinity which is revealed and experienced through Him, which always remain the essential focus of Orthodox liturgical worship.

Holy Tradition and Fidelity to the Faith

Not only the clergy but Orthodox laity as well consider themselves personally responsible to guard and protect these sacred ways of worship. The laity are also conscious of their God-given calling to keep this precious liturgical life—and indeed all the various practices of Holy Tradition—pure and intact. They are intensely aware of their divine duty to pass them on unchanged, just as they have received them from their forefathers, and not only to their own children but indeed to all future generations of the Orthodox Church.

Such a sense of duty is reflected in the words of St. John Damascene, who writes in the eighth century in defense of the veneration of holy icons, "We will not remove the age-old landmarks which our fathers have set, but we keep the tradition we have received. For if we begin to erode the foundations of the Church even a little, in no time at all the whole edifice will fall to the ground."[41]

---

[40] Cf. G. Mantzaridis, *Time and Man*, p. 63.
[41] St. John Damascene, *On the Divine Images*, 2. 12, trans. D. Anderson, Crestwood, 1980, p. 60; PG 94, 1297B.

This unique Orthodox mind-set—this 'catholic consciousness'—continues to be manifested within the life of the Church today. This mentality often finds expression through the curious phenomenon of what has affectionately become known in America as '*yiayia* theology' (or depending on your ethnic persuasion, '*babushka* theology'). In Greek and Russian, *yiayia* and *babushka* mean 'grandmother' or 'grandma'—that is to say, 'grandma theology'.

This particular mind-set takes its name from the fact that it is often the elderly and aged women of most any given Orthodox parish, usually from the 'old country', who make a unique contribution to the local community. In the United States, they exhibit not so much that superstitious mentality often associated with village life in the rural settings of Eastern Europe, but rather a conservative and safeguarding perspective, which they are quite consciously passing on to the next generation of the 'new' world.

They keep their eyes always open, seeking out the infractions of anyone who might defy the time-honored traditions of the Orthodox Church. They are quick to correct the conduct of the newly ordained deacon who may not be swinging his censer in the appropriate Orthodox manner, or the new convert who is still a bit haphazard in the way he crosses himself.

At times their actions can be construed as rude and rather crude. These include remarks to a first time visitor who has the audacity to cross his legs when allowed within an Orthodox Church; or the chastising of the teenage girl who dares to wear her skirt a bit too short;

or the reprimand of the young mother whose toddlers are talking and walking around during the reading of the Holy Gospel.

Such examples are brought forth to show that regardless of the extent to which the Orthodox believer actually comprehends the deeper spiritual truths of the ways of Holy Tradition, he or she nevertheless feels *responsible* to contribute, in whatever way possible, to maintaining the full integrity of the Orthodox Faith.

Fr. John Meyendorff comments on this unique Orthodox mind-set from both a psychological as well as a historical perspective:

> An Orthodox generally conceives his Christianity as an integral whole which finds its expression in doctrinal convictions as well as in liturgical worship and in whatever attitude he takes as a Christian. ... Its psychological root is in ... the positive sense of *responsibility* that an Orthodox usually has for the *integrity* of his faith. He is, consciously or unconsciously, but rightly, aware of the fact that all acts of worship have some doctrinal implications and that true Christianity is to be taken as a whole set of beliefs and attitudes.[42]

He goes on to describe how this "formal and ritualistic conservatism" found among Orthodox believers provided a fundamental role in the preservation of the Faith,

---

[42] J. Meyendorff, *Living Tradition*, Crestwood, 1978, pp. 21-22.

especially in Eastern Europe where many Orthodox countries were once dominated by foreign occupation.[43]

This "formal and ritualistic conservatism" as embodied in the spiritual lives of our beloved babushka and yiayia is not necessarily a bad thing. In spite of some of its shortcomings, such convictions can nevertheless continue to provide a positive contribution.

This is especially relevant for the Orthodox in America, Australia and western Europe, as we proceed into the twenty-first century continually confronted with the 'western captivity'[44] of the Orthodox mind.

Regardless of one's level of spiritual progress or ascetic experience, there should grow organically within the consciousness of every Orthodox believer certain seeds of virtue which inherently seek and strive to safeguard the sacred treasure of Tradition. Ignited inside every Orthodox soul is an ember that slowly grows into a flame, which needs to be fanned and fueled so that it never fades away. This holy fire—this sacred light of Holy Tradition—becomes a most precious possession. The Orthodox Christian is called to protect, preserve and pass it on pure and whole, keeping it intact in its entirety for each and every believer who comes after him.

This "formal and ritualistic conservatism", this catholic consciousness, this innate responsibility felt by every lay believer, lies embedded within the very life of the Church and it manifests her catholic nature.

---

[43] Cf. ibid., p. 22.

[44] See G. Florovsky, *Aspects of Church History*, Vaduz, 1987, pp. 157-182.

According to Elder Vasileios, "The responsibility of the laity ... reveals the catholic character of the truth and its vital place within the body of the Church. Through the responsibility that weighs upon the laity, the faithful partake, in practice and not merely in theory, in the life of the Church."[45]

Maybe this is why some of our yiayias and babushkas instinctively seek after anything that may appear to detract, diminish or degrade the catholic fullness of the life of our Church. They are quite conscious of their calling and thus they are always ready and willing to point out any errant indiscretion involving even the most seemingly insignificant practice of Church life.

This common catholic life of Holy Tradition obviously provides a unifying factor that unites us as a community of believers. And it is this sacramental community which serves as the spiritual sphere wherein we grow into the full stature of our lives in Christ: "The universal responsibility of the laity ... leads everyone as a community and as persons to spiritual maturity and adulthood in Christ. ... We are bound together by the common faith which, in accordance with tradition, each of us has found and finds personally through the exercise of his own responsibility..."[46]

It is not just parish priests and lay believers alone who are conscious of this responsibility. Nor is it the case that our yiayias and babushkas have a monopoly on catholic consciousness.

---

[45] Archim. Vasileios, *Hymn of Entry*, p. 49.
[46] Ibid., p. 50.

There is another essential element within the life of the Church, another vital organ that not only preserves the life of Holy Tradition, but in fact animates, enhances and indeed uniquely incarnates this life within the Body of Christ.

Holy Tradition and Orthodox Monasticism

Just as the Orthodox Church does not exist apart from the life of Holy Tradition, so the Church does not exist apart from Orthodox monasticism.

Monasticism embodies the innate ascetic spirit, the integral liturgical life and the unending pursuit of prayer which compose and characterize the life of the Orthodox Church. Monasticism lies at the inner heart of the Church by virtue of the fact that it constitutes complete commitment to the commandments of Christ. It strives for nothing less than total devotion to undivided discipleship. The way of monasticism, traditionally referred to as the 'university of the desert', serves as a school wherein one commences the ultimate education in the science of the hidden ways of the human heart; the font wherein the abundant life of Holy Tradition comes alive in all its fullness.

Monasticism has always provided a vital ministry within the Orthodox Church. Even from a purely historical perspective, the impact of monasticism on the life of the Church is remarkable. Its far-reaching influence is vast and wide. Fr. Meyendorff comments on its impact, due not only to its sheer numbers, but also to the fact that from the sixth century, according to canon law, anyone elected to become a bishop had to be a monk:

> Numbering thousands in Constantinople itself, in the major cities, and in practically every corner of the Byzantine world, the monks consistently opposed doctrinal compromises; they defended a rigorous orthodoxy... Thus Byzantine spirituality and much of the Byzantine liturgy were shaped by monks. ... The numerical, spiritual, and intellectual strength of Byzantine monasticism was the decisive factor which preserved in the Church the fundamental eschatological dimension of the Christian faith.[47]

Some see monasticism as a form of retreat from the Church's ministry to the world. But this is not the case. Just as monasticism does not exist outside of the Church, neither does it lie outside of—nor does it seek to escape from—the pain and suffering engulfing the fallen world in which we live. Orthodox monasticism embraces this pain. It embodies this suffering. And it baptizes and transfigures them within the light and life of the victory of the resurrected Christ.[48]

---

[47] J. Meyendorff, *Byzantine Theology,* New York, 1974, p. 6.
[48] Cf. G. Mantzaridis, "The monk does not turn away from suffering, but adopts a positive attitude towards it. ... In suffering he perceives the means of his spiritual purification and his preparation for the Kingdom of God. ... The monk lives the Kingdom of God within himself eschatologically, in that already, in this present life he has a foretaste of the joy and triumph of the Kingdom.

Rather than running away from the pain and problems of the world, the monk dedicates his entire life to living out their ultimate solution. He picks up his cross and is crucified every day of his life: "If anyone desires to come after Me, let him deny himself, and take up his cross daily, and follow Me. For whoever desires to save his life will lose it, but whoever loses his life for My sake will save it."[49] His very life expresses the certainty that all of its problems, with all of its pain and suffering—even death itself—is ultimately overcome by Christ and *in* Christ: "We are hard-pressed on every side, yet not crushed; we are perplexed, but not in despair ... always carrying about in the body the dying of the Lord Jesus, that the life of Jesus also may be manifested in our body."[50] Through the ascetic life of Holy Tradition the Orthodox monk dies daily, yet lives truly the abundant *life* in Jesus Christ: "Dying, yet behold we live."[51]

The sole goal of the Orthodox monk is to penetrate, as far as he or she is able, into the boundless depths of the life in Christ through the Church's liturgical life of prayer. A monk becomes a 'liturgical being',

---

The transformation of sorrow into joy, of which Christ spoke to His disciples [John 16. 20-22] is the monk's daily experience. The term 'joyful sorrow', which ascetics generally use to denote the experience of this eschatological transcendence of suffering, is possibly the most expressive image of the entire ascetic life." *The Deification of Man*, trans. L. Sherrard, Crestwood, 1984, pp. 76-77.

[49] Luke 9. 23, 24.

[50] 2 Cor. 4. 8-11.

[51] 2 Cor. 6. 9.

who is devoted to the daily liturgical life of the Church and to the pursuit of unceasing prayer.[52]

The Orthodox monk vows unconditionally to dedicate his entire earthly life—until the very day of his death—to the exclusive pursuit of this holy way of life. The life of Holy Tradition becomes his sole source of nourishment, *in* which he is nurtured, and *around* which his whole world revolves.

This life of Tradition remains not only his ultimate focus, but likewise the very locus of his life. He personally lives this Tradition through his daily experience. Holy Tradition thus truly comes alive through the daily life of the Orthodox monk. His goal in life is the constant pursuit of any and all of the various forms of prayer found within the life of the Church, whether liturgical and corporate or personal and private, since prayer is the foundation of our lives in Christ.

One of the marks of the Orthodox Church is holiness. Where there is unceasing prayer—pure prayer of the inner heart—there is the fullness of the grace of the Holy Spirit.[53] And where the fullness of the grace of the Holy Spirit is found, there is the true life of the Holy Church in all her glory—the abundant life of the One, Holy, Catholic and Apostolic Church of Christ.[54]

---

[52] Cf. 1 Thess. 5. 17.

[53] Cf. J. Romanides, *Patristic Theology*, The Dalles, 2008, pp. 203-209.

[54] Cf. J. Romanides, *An Outline of Orthodox Patristic Dogmatics*, pp. 77-81.

I recall asking one of our students who formerly belonged to a non-canonical jurisdiction why he left, and what it was exactly that led him to the canonical Orthodox Church. Is there really any difference other than such basic issues as the validity of the new calendar and ecumenical dialogue? After all, don't we uphold the same dogmas, share the same liturgical life, venerate the same Saints and celebrate the same sacraments? If we hold all these elements of Holy Tradition in common, why then the need to become canonical? I genuinely wanted to know what prompted his conversion. So I asked him whole-heartedly, "Just what was it that was missing from your non-canonical experience, that brought you to the canonical Church?" He looked at me, pondering intently. He replied with one word— "holiness." He then went on to confide how it was the lives and writings of our contemporary holy elders that led him to the canonical Orthodox Church.

It is lives such as theirs, springing forth within the 'desert' of the Orthodox monastery, which brings to life the full fruits of Holy Tradition. By virtue of its lifelong vow of unwavering dedication to the Church's authentic spirit of prayer, asceticism and the fullness of her liturgical life in Christ, Orthodox monasticism innately constitutes and conserves the organic wholeness of Holy Tradition in all of its splendor and glory: "Entering through faith into the life of the universal Church, the monk becomes co-possessor of her boundless riches, and his own personal experience acquires an absolutely authentic character."[55]

Now it must be plainly stated, that this by no means implies that the spiritual life of the lay believer living within society is somehow inferior or less significant than that of the Orthodox monk. Within the life of the Orthodox Church both monk and layman seek the same goal. Both pursue the same life in Christ. Both partake in the same grace of the Holy Spirit. Both are full-fledged members of the same holy Church. Both ways of life provide the possibility to acquire the same spiritual virtues.

A classic example illustrating this truth is attributed to *The Sayings of the Desert Fathers* (*The Gerontikon*), where St. Anthony the Great is portrayed as asking God to reveal to him the level of spiritual perfection he had attained. St. Anthony himself—the Father of Orthodox Monasticism—is astonished to learn that rather than an aged ascetic with years of experience living in the desert, the Lord leads him rather to a simple cobbler, married and living within the city of Alexandria:

> When St. Anthony announced that the Lord had sent him to be taught by the cobbler, the later replied: 'I, Abba, have never done anything good, I only struggle to keep the holy teachings of the Gospel. And further, I try never to forget my shortcomings and my spiritual fruitlessness. Therefore, as I work during the day, I always think and say to myself:

---

[55] Archim. Sophrony, *Saint Silouan the Athonite*, trans. R. Edmonds, Essex, 1991, p. 89.

'O wretched man, all will be saved and only
you will remain fruitless. Because of your
sin, you will never be worthy to see His Holy
Face'. St. Anthony, greatly edified, upon leav-
ing, reflected, 'Humility! This therefore is the
quickest path to the gate of Paradise. Humility is the robe in which God clothed Himself
and came to earth as man.'[56]

This spiritual gem, itself a small token taken from
the treasure-chest of Holy Tradition, clearly shows how
the greatest teachers of the desert themselves are the
first to emphasize how monasticism does not have any
kind of a monopoly on the acquisition of spiritual virtues.

Commenting on this passage Elder Vasileios, himself from Mount Athos, observes, "This cobbler is now
in the position of St. Anthony. St. Anthony is not as
great as a cobbler: one who is unknown, unrecognized
by the world, and yet living in the same holiness of life.
That is the greatest thing. You might say, 'You are on
the Holy Mountain, a place holy and sacred, but we are
in the world. So, you are in a coveted position'. But it is
not so. The great fact is that God is love and that we are
Orthodox Christians. Whether we find ourselves on the
Holy Mountain or in the world, it is the same thing."[57]

---

[56] *The Gerontikon*, trans. from *The Orthodox Word* 279, Platina,
2011, p. 159.
[57] Archim. Vasileios, 'Everything is Prayer', *The Orthodox Word*
279, Platina, 2011, p. 159.

The Elder concludes:

Therefore, if someone says, 'I am in the world; I am at a lower level of spiritual life; you are in the monastery on the Holy Mountain; you are on a higher level', I don't see that as being correct. We see from an Orthodox view that God judges things differently. ... Therefore, we are all together; the monks who are struggling on the Mountain and the laypeople who are ... struggling in the world. We are all together; we are one. Let us make the sign of the Cross and go forward with life. And great is the one who is humble.[58]

---

[58] Ibid., pp. 162-163, 170.

Life in Christ—the Content and Core of Holy Tradition

Having discussed these preliminary issues we now move on to examine the deeper theological implications of the life of Holy Tradition and its impact on our own spiritual lives. The first and foremost aspect to be considered is its direct Christological perspective. As was mentioned earlier, there is an intrinsic and integral relationship between Holy Tradition and the life in Christ.

Based on this Christological context, many Orthodox theologians approach Holy Tradition from a personal perspective, defining it in terms of experiential participation in the Church's constant and continuous life in Christ. For example, Fr. Dumitru Staniloae defines Tradition as "a lived experience of one and the same relationship with Christ, experienced by the Church in the time of the Apostles, a continuous experience of the whole mystery revealed in Christ. In this way Tradition is a living reality, it is the uninterrupted life of the Church, and as such it can neither be reduced, nor increased, nor changed in its essence."[59]

Elsewhere Fr. Staniloae describes Holy Tradition as the "identity of the knowledge of Christ;" as "the totality of the various ways by which Christ passes over into the reality of human lives under the form of the

---

[59] D. Staniloae, 'The Orthodox Conception of Tradition and the Development of Doctrine', *Sobornost* 5. 9, 1969, pp. 653-654.

Church;" and he refers to Christ as "the unchanged content of tradition."[60]

Fr. John Chryssavgis likewise identifies Christ with the content of Holy Tradition. Writing from more of a liturgical perspective he adds, "There is, in the context of the Liturgy, a virtual identity between Christ and Tradition, between Christ who is not only past but present and future. ... In the Liturgy it is Christ who is handed down and who is being received. It is he who is the content of Tradition, not so much as he who is handed down to us from the past, but as he to whom we hand ourselves over in the living present of the Church."[61]

Other theologians share similar views. Prof. Scouteris likewise directly identifies Holy Tradition with Christ Himself.[62] Prof. Mantzaridis also refers to Christ as the 'core' of Holy Tradition.[63] And Metropolitan Kallistos (Ware) refers to Holy Tradition as "a personal encounter with Christ in the Holy Spirit."[64] In this context of the continuous presence of Christ as the core of Holy Tradition, one recalls the words of the Lord Himself when He promises His disciples, "Lo, I am with you always, even to the end of the age."[65]

---

[60] D. Staniloae, *The Experience of God*, Brookline, 1994, pp. 46, 48.

[61] J. Chryssavgis, 'The Liturgy as Tradition and Tradition as Liturgy', *Sobornost* 7. 2, 1985, pp. 18-19.

[62] Cf. C. Scouteris, 'Paradosis: The Orthodox Understanding of Tradition', p. 131.

[63] Cf. G. Mantzaridis, *Time and Man*, p. 62.

[64] Cf. T. Ware, *The Orthodox Church*, p. 198.

[65] Matt. 28. 20.

Fr. John Romanides adds a further dimension to this Christological perspective of Holy Tradition. For him, the core of Tradition is not simply Christ, but it is the transmission of the Church's therapeutic method of spiritual healing *through* Christ and *in* Christ. More specifically, the ultimate core and heart of Holy Tradition is the transmission of the therapeutic *life* in Christ, consisting of the experience of the three stages of purification, illumination and deification (or *theosis*):

> This therapeutic method and course of treatment that the Orthodox tradition has to offer, has been handed down from generation to generation by people who, having reached the state of illumination or *theosis*, became therapists for others. We are not talking here simply about knowledge that has been transmitted through books, but about experience—both the experience of illumination and the experience of *theosis*—which has been handed down successively, from one person to another. ... And this tradition ... of illumination and *theosis* ... is the core of the Orthodox tradition. In other words, the core of the Orthodox tradition is this transmission of the experience of illumination and *theosis* from one generation to the next. ... This curative course of treatment is the very fiber of Orthodox tradition.[66]

---

[66] J. Romanides, *Patristic Theology*, trans. Hieromonk Alexios (Trader), pp. 41-42, 48. Cf. J. Romanides, *An Outline of Orthodox Patristic Dogmatics*, pp. 81-85.

Holy Tradition: The Life of the Holy Spirit within the Holy Church

Following this Christological approach to Holy Tradition as the ecclesial experience of the fullness of the life in Christ, other theologians offer a pneumato-logical perspective as well. They refer to the integral relationship between Holy Tradition and the direct experience of the grace-filled life of the Holy Spirit within the Church.

The classic definition is presented by Vladimir Lossky. Writing in the context of experiencing revealed Truth, he refers to Holy Tradition as *"the life of the Holy Spirit in the Church*, communicating to each member of the Body of Christ the faculty of hearing, of receiving, of knowing the Truth ..."[67] Elsewhere he adds, "Tradition ... is the unique mode of receiving the revealed Truth, of recognizing it in its scriptural, dogmatic, iconographic and other expressions and also of expressing it anew."[68]

This relationship between Holy Tradition and the experience of revealed Truth is based on the Lord's words referring to the sending of the Holy Spirit, "I still have many things to say to you, but you cannot bear

---

[67] V. Lossky, *In the Image and Likeness of God*, p. 152 (emphasis mine).
[68] Ibid., p. 168.

them now. However, when He, the Spirit of Truth, has come, He will guide you into all truth."[69]

Commenting on this relationship of Holy Tradition and the grace of the Holy Spirit, Elder Sophrony adds, "For [St. Silouan] the life of the Church meant life in the Holy Spirit, and Sacred Tradition the unceasing action of the Holy Spirit in her. Sacred Tradition, as the eternal and immutable dwelling of the Holy Spirit in the Church, lies at the very root of her being, and so encompasses her life ..."[70]

The ecclesial life of Holy Tradition can thus be considered as a charismatic, even a 'pentecostal' experience. Expanding on this particular theme Fr. Florovsky offers the following reflections: "Ultimately, tradition is a continuity of the abiding presence of the Holy Spirit in the Church, a continuity of Divine guidance and illumination;"[71] "Tradition is the inner, mystical *memory of the Church*. It is, above all, the 'unity of the Spirit', the unity and continuity of the spiritual experience and the life of grace. It is the living connection with the day of Pentecost, the day when the Holy Spirit descended into the world as the 'Spirit of Truth';" "Faithfulness to Tradition is ... a participation in Pentecost, and Tradition represents a fulfillment of Pentecost."[72]

---

[69] John 16. 13.

[70] Archim. Sophrony, *St. Silouan the Athonite*, p. 87.

[71] G. Florovsky, *Bible, Church, Tradition: An Eastern Orthodox View*, Belmont, 1972, p. 106.

[72] G. Florovsky, *Creation and Redemption*, pp. 36-37 and 194-195.

Further emphasizing this pentecostal perspective of Holy Tradition, Prof. Scouteris reiterates the significance of the continual presence of the indwelling of the Holy Spirit within the life of the Church, "The descent of the Holy Spirit, understood as *paradosis* (a 'handing-over' or 'giving-over') and *enoikesis* (indwelling) in the body of the Church, ensures the preservation of the truth and the new life. The Holy Spirit is given over (*paradidetai*) to the Church. ... Pentecost is not an event belonging to the past: rather it is a continuous *present* in the life of the Church."[73]

---

[73] C. Scouteris, 'Paradosis: The Orthodox Understanding of Tradition', p. 132 (emphasis mine).

The Life of Tradition and Trinitarian Life

Holy Tradition thus has a unique and experiential life which is known only by *living* it within the Orthodox Church. The life of Holy Tradition is not an objective entity that is meant to be externally examined, dissected and discussed from outside the life of the Church. Its life is a phenomenon which has its being only when it is freely *chosen*; when it is personified through free choice; when it is embodied in human persons through the synergy of human freedom and the divine grace of the Holy Spirit.

By participating in the life of Holy Tradition, we participate in the grace-filled life of the Holy Spirit. And as an extension of this, by participating in this life of divine grace, we participate in the divine life of the Holy Trinity. And it is this participation, through divine grace, in the divine life and love of the Holy Trinity toward which Holy Tradition tends and takes us: "Tradition is ... the life of the whole Trinity as revealed by Christ and testified by the Holy Spirit. Tradition both ... begins from the Holy Trinity and ends in the Holy Trinity."[74]

Holy Tradition is brought to life—indeed it *gives* life—only within this framework of personal experience. In this experiential context of Trinitarian life and love Professor Scouteris writes: "Thus, both within the

---

[74] G. Bebis, 'The Concept of Tradition in the Fathers of the Church', *The Greek Orthodox Theological Review*, 15, 1, 1970, p. 29.

relations between the three divine hypostases as well as within the Church (which in turn is an image of the communion of the Trinity) God's love is manifested as *paradosis*, as a constant outpouring."[75]

Through our participation therefore, in the life of Holy Tradition, we are united not only with each other, but by divine grace, we participate in the divine life of the Heavenly Kingdom: "The mystery of unity, as the Church lives and understands it, is the Kingdom of the Father and the Son and the Holy Spirit, 'through which as a unifying force we are united; the distinctions which divide us are laid aside in a manner surpassing this world, and we are brought together in God-like oneness and union imitating that of God'."[76]

---

[75] C. Scouteris, 'Paradosis: The Orthodox Understanding of Tradition', p. 132. Cf. G. Mantzaridis, "The Church's body, which is the very body of Christ, reveals the mystery of the triadic communion in the world and encompasses man within it. Just as each person of the Holy Trinity exists integrally by itself, each also exists wholly in each of the other persons of the Trinity, and furthermore exists wholly in the totality of the triadic communion. Thus, Christ—and similarly the Trinitarian God—exists totally in himself, exists wholly in every believer, and also exists wholly in the total communion of the faithful, in the Church." *Orthodox Spiritual Life*, p. 62.

[76] Archim. Vasileios, *Hymn of Entry*, p. 48. Cf. St. Dionysius the Areopagite, *On the Divine Names* 1. 4; PG 3, 589D.

Holy Tradition and Holy Scripture

With this theological basis as a foundation, we move on to discuss the place of Holy Scripture within Holy Tradition. In the nascent Church, it was the Jewish Bible, or what we now refer to as the 'Old Testament', which served as the sacred Scriptures for the Apostles and their immediate successors. And it was the Hebrew Bible from which our Lord Himself quoted and on which He based His own teaching. However, there soon came into existence, together with this 'Old Testament' canon of writings, a preliminary form of another set of sacred writings, which the Church would soon consider as her 'New Testament'.

Although the 'Old Testament' retained its place of special honor as sacred Scripture within the nascent Church, other sayings which were passed down orally were also considered as sacred. Obviously, the words of the Lord held the highest authority: "Heaven and earth will pass away, but My words will by no means pass away."[77]

Even though Christ Himself wrote nothing, His Apostles did indeed eventually write down His words, teachings, parables and prophecies. Even from a secular perspective, it is amazing to consider how Christ instituted His Church without any written documents of His own. He has not left even one word in His own writing. The Lord passed His teachings to His Apostles orally.

---

[77] Matt. 24. 35.

But as the Church expanded, and as the original Apostles of the Lord began passing away, the need arose to write down His teachings and the events of His life in order to pass them on to their disciples.

It is interesting to note that the phrase 'It is written' is used by the Lord Himself when introducing quotations from His own sacred Scripture, the Hebrew Bible or our 'Old Testament'; as for example when He answers Satan at His Temptation in the wilderness.[78] This same phrase 'It is written' is also used by the Apostles in their letters to the earliest Christian communities when introducing Old Testament quotations.[79] In the generation after the Apostles, that is to say, in the writings of *their* disciples, that is the disciples of the original Apostles who are known as 'Apostolic Fathers', the words 'It is written' are also used to introduce the sayings of the Lord.[80]

This shows how at this very early date, the words of the Lord were considered just as equally important and carried the same authority as those of the Hebrew Bible, if not more.[81] Elsewhere in the Apostolic Fathers, the words of the Lord are clearly equated with Scripture.[82] And not only the Gospels, but the letters of the Apostles themselves were also important for the life and ordering of the earliest churches. In the Second Epistle of Peter, the letters of Paul are considered as of

---

[78] Cf. Matt. 4. 4, 7, 10.

[79] E.g., Rom. 3. 4, 10; 8. 36; 9. 13, 33, et al.

[80] E.g., *The Epistle of Barnabas* 4. 14. Cf. B. Lohse, *A Short History of Christian Doctrine*, Philadelphia, 1985, p. 27.

[81] Cf. B. Lohse, ibid.

[82] E. g., *2 Clement* 2. 4.

equal value with the 'rest of the Scriptures', that is, with the books of the 'Old Testament'.[83] The fact that the letters of the Apostles were read within the setting of liturgical worship shows that they also obviously played a crucial role in the preaching and teaching ministry of the Church as well.

The authority of these apostolic writings, which would eventually become our New Testament, is based on the fact that they were written by eyewitnesses of the resurrected Christ. And once these eyewitnesses passed away, it then became impossible to produce any 'new' apostolic writings based on such eyewitness accounts. The Church, however, had the power and authority to decide which writings were in fact based on this authentic apostolic witness, and thus merited inclusion into her eventual New Testament canon.[84]

It is also important to point out that the Church considered apostolic authenticity in terms of the *content* of particular writings, not so much in terms as whether the book was actually composed from the hand of one of the Twelve. For example, Mark and Luke were not members of the original Twelve Apostles.[85] Yet their Gospels were always considered as 'canonical' in the early Church, since their teaching is based on the witness and preaching of the Apostles Peter and Paul, respectively.[86] The same holds true with regard to the Epistle to the Hebrews. While some writers in the early

---

[83] Cf. 2 Peter 3. 15, 16.

[84] Cf. J. Meyendorff, *Living Tradition*, p. 14.

[85] See Matt. 10. 2-4.

[86] Cf. St. Irenaeus, *Against Heresies* 3. 1. 1; PG7, 845A and Eusebius, *Ecclesiastical History* 5. 8; PG20, 449A.

Church questioned whether it was actually composed by the Apostle Paul himself, no one sought to reject it from the New Testament canon, since the content was obviously covered by the authority of Paul.[87]

Another element playing a decisive role when considering which books would be included in the Church's new canon of Scripture was whether or not they were read within her liturgical life of worship.[88] This shows how the New Testament canon did not somehow pre-date the Church, nor did it somehow arise from outside of the Church. It was the Church which produced her New Testament canon, and not the New Testament which produced the Christian Church.

Commenting on the teaching of St. Silouan of Mount Athos and his understanding of this inherent unity and organic wholeness of Holy Tradition and Holy Scripture, Elder Sophrony teaches, "The life of the Church meant life in the Holy Spirit, and Sacred Tradition the unceasing action of the Holy Spirit in her. Sacred Tradition, as the eternal and immutable dwelling of the Holy Spirit in the Church, lies at the very root of her being, and so encompasses her life that even the very Scriptures come to be but one of its forms."[89]

Elder Sophrony continues:

Suppose that for some reason the Church were to be bereft of all of her books, the Old

---

[87] Cf. J. Meyendorff, *Living Tradition*, pp. 14-15.
[88] Cf. C. Scouteris, *Ἱστορία Δογμάτων*, vol. 1, Athens, 1998, p. 495.
[89] Archim. Sophrony, *St. Silouan the Athonite*, p. 87.

and New Testaments ... Sacred Tradition
would restore the Scriptures, not word for
word, perhaps—the verbal form might be different—but in essence the new Scriptures
would be the expression of that same 'faith
which was once delivered unto the saints'.
They would be the expression of the one and
only Holy Spirit continuously active in the
Church, her foundation and her very sub-
stance.[90]

Clearly, from an Orthodox perspective, the New Testament organically sprang up from within the very life of
the Church, and more specifically, from within her liturgical and sacramental life.[91]

Another important point to be made here is the
proper Orthodox understanding of the organic unity of
the Old and New Testaments. The New Testament was
never considered as abolishing the Old Testament, but
rather as fulfilling it. The words of our Lord Himself
sum up the Church's attitude toward the Old Testament, "Do not think that I came to destroy the Law or
the Prophets. I did not come to destroy but to fulfill."[92]
In fact in the time of the early Church, it was often the
heretical groups who did not identify with the teachings
and experiences of the Patriarchs and Prophets of the
Old Testament.

---

[90] Ibid., pp. 87-88.
[91] Cf. C. Scouteris, Ἱστορία Δογμάτων, vol. 1, p. 495.
[92] Matt. 5. 17.

In the eyes of the Church, the Old Testament and the New Testament are seen as an inherent whole. The Church alone possesses the proper interpretation of Holy Scriptures and especially the right understanding of the Old Testament prophecies, since it was Christ Who fulfilled these prophecies.[93] Fr. Florovsky writes:

> The student of public worship in the Eastern Orthodox Church would be impressed by the amount of Old Testament references, hints and images, in all offices and hymns. The unity of the two Testaments is stressed throughout. ... On great festivals numerous lessons from the Old Testament are appointed and actually read to stress that Christian perfection was but a consummation of what was pre-figured and foreshadowed or even directly predicted of old.[94]

The Old Testament thus plays a fundamental role in not only the Church's experience and expression of her theology and spiritual life, but also in her liturgical life.

Having discussed the organic wholeness of the Old and New Testaments, it is also helpful to comment on the origin of the term 'Old Testament', as well as the final formation of the Church's New Testament Canon. Among the first to use the term 'Old Testament' in reference to the Jewish Scriptures was St. Melito, Bishop of Sardis, who died around 190 at the end of the second

---

[93] Cf. G. Florovsky, *Aspects of Church History*, Belmont, 1975, p. 31.
[94] Ibid., p. 37.

century.[95] Since he uses the word 'Old' for the Hebrew Bible it is not difficult to assume that in contrast to this, the term 'New Testament' was also used around this time to refer to the newly formed collection of sacred Scriptures of the Christian Church.[96] Most scholars agree that the final fixing of the New Testament canon, with its 27 official books still in use today, is attributed to St. Athanasius the Great and his famous *Festal Epistle* 39, written in the year 367.

Before the compilation of this official canon and its general acceptance throughout the Church, various other collections were in circulation, which obviously paved the way for this final and authoritative canon of New Testament Scriptures.[97] Near the end of the second century, probably around 170-180, a document from Rome referred to as the Muratorian Canon is perhaps the most ancient compilation of New Testament writings which lists all the commonly accepted books except Hebrews, James and 1 and 2 Peter. The canonicity of some other epistles remained in dispute for quite some time, including Jude, 2 and 3 John, as well as the Book of Revelation.[98]

The Muratorian Canon witnesses to the fact that already by the end of the second century, the most important writings of the New Testament, including the four Gospels and the letters of Paul, were recognized by

---

[95] Cf. Eusebius, *Ecclesiastical History* 4. 26; PG20, 396C.

[96] Cf. T. Stylianopoulos, *The New Testament: An Orthodox Perspective*, Brookline, 1997, p. 27.

[97] Cf. C. Scouteris, Ἱστορία Δογμάτων, vol. 1, p. 495.

[98] Cf. T. Stylianopoulos, ibid.

the Church as her 'New Testament' Scriptures, even though she still did not have an exact and universally accepted configuration of a New Testament 'canon'.[99]

It is clear then that the very existence of the New Testament writings presupposes the existence of the One, Holy, Catholic and Apostolic Church. The New Testament and the Church can never be separated or isolated from one another. They are interdependent and mutually inclusive. And with the final formation of her New Testament canon, the Church had at her disposal a sure, significant and universally accepted Scriptural foundation on which to base her theological doctrines, not only for use in the instruction of her own faithful, but also in the face of countering heretical teachings as well.[100]

---

[99] Cf. C. Scouteris, *Ἱστορία Δογμάτων*, vol. 1, p. 496.
[100] Cf. ibid.

Marcion

The person of Marcion presents an interesting character within the annals of the ancient Church. He was an arch-heretic who, in order to defend his own heretical teachings, was actually the first to fix a definite New Testament canon.[101] He provided a major motivation that led the Church to speed up the process of defining her own canon of New Testament writings.

His heretical teachings and the church he established are interesting to examine. It allows us to see how such heresiarchs, or founders of heretical groups, arrived at their erroneous opinions and how their teachings differed from and threatened the spiritual well-being of the Church. This will help to understand why the Church was compelled to react as she did, by formally recognizing and officially proclaiming that such heretical teachers and their followers have in fact cut *themselves* off from the therapeutic experience of the Church and thus separated themselves from the apostolic life of Holy Tradition. Marcion's heretical movement was not the only one facing the early Church. Yet he was indeed a major threat and the wide-spread impact of his heresy shows how dangerous it is to act and operate outside the apostolic teachings of Holy Tradition.

Marcion was a successful shipowner who died around the year 160. His father was a bishop of Sinope

---

[101] E. g., P. Chrestou, Ἑλληνικὴ Πατρολογία, vol. 2, Thessaloniki, 1978, p. 181.

in Pontus who excommunicated his own son, allegedly on the grounds of corrupting a virgin.[102] In 140 Marcion was in Rome where he began to attract adherents to his heresy. In 144 the Church of Rome excommunicated him as well on account of the divergence of his theological views from those of Holy Tradition.

As a charismatic teacher and wealthy administrator, Marcion created small groups of dedicated followers who helped spread his teachings throughout the Roman Empire. The fact that so many patristic authors wrote against him testifies to his achievements. From a theological standpoint, in the second half of the second century, it was the followers of Marcion who posed the greatest threat to the Church in terms of maintaining the orthodoxy of her apostolic teachings.[103]

Many diverse influences from outside of Holy Tradition played a fundamental role in the formulation of Marcion's heresy. These include various elements from Gnostic teachings, such as God's absolute transcendence and even estrangement from the created world, the inherent impurity of the material creation, as well as extreme forms of asceticism.

---

[102] Prof. Chrestou questions the validity of this charge, due to the fact that among all the major theologians who wrote against him, it is recorded in only one source and not collaborated elsewhere. Furthermore, he claims that since Marcion advocated an extreme form of abstinence and asceticism, this also makes this charge suspect. Chrestou believes it may rather be some kind of a reference to the fact that he did not uphold the virgin birth of Christ as did those who followed the apostolic teaching of Holy Tradition. See ibid., pp. 178 and 183.

[103] Cf. *The Oxford Dictionary of the Christian Church*, Oxford, 1997, pp. 1033-1034.

He also fell into docetism. Docetism is a heretical tendency that basically denies the full humanity of Christ. It is a rejection of the true Incarnation of the Son of God. Based on platonic dualism, which upheld a separation and alienation between the spiritual and material worlds, the heresy of docetism held that Christ, since He is God, could not have truly become man nor assumed a genuine material human body; neither did he suffer nor die on the Cross. Rather, he only *appeared* to take on human flesh; His body was only a phantasm; and His suffering and death on the Cross were in appearance only; they did not really happen.[104]

Obviously, this is a complete rejection of basic Orthodox doctrine concerning the Incarnation of Christ. It is also a denial of the Church's teaching of salvation and sanctification as experienced by the Apostles and Saints—summed up in the words of St. Athanasius the Great, 'God became man, so that man can become divine'.[105] The logic of docetism would lead to the conclusion that since Christ is not truly human, there can be no true union between God and man. There can be no real communion between the Creator and His creation. Therefore man cannot become holy as the Church knows from her experience, nor can the material creation be sanctified in Christ. Such teaching contradicts the ecclesial experience of Holy Tradition. Docetism is not only a denial of the Incarnation of God—it is also a

---

[104] Cf. *Θρησκευτικὴ καὶ 'Ηθικὴ 'Εγκυκλοπαιδεία*, vol. 5, Athens, 1964, pp. 149-151.

[105] See St. Athanasius, *On the Incarnation* 54; PG 25, 192B. Cf. St. Irenaeus, *Against Heresies* 3. 10. 2; PG 7, 873B. Refer also to 1 Peter 1. 15, 16 and 2 Peter 1. 4.

denial of the deification of man—a repudiation of man's hope for holiness in Christ.

Docetism was not so much a distinct and organized heresy with a systematic teaching of its own. Rather it was more of a tendency that infected other heretical movements, including Marcionism. The heresy of docetism spread so extensively and left such a vast impact that even as early as the writings of the Apostle and Evangelist St. John the Theologian, believers are warned of its danger. He teaches in his epistles: "By this you know the Spirit of God: Every spirit that confesses that Jesus Christ has come in the flesh is of God, and every spirit that does not confess that Jesus Christ has come in the flesh is not of God. And this is the spirit of the Antichrist, which you have heard was coming, and is now already in the world."[106] And elsewhere, "For many deceivers have gone out into the world who do not confess Jesus Christ as coming in the flesh. This is a deceiver and an antichrist."[107]

This is obviously one reason why Marcion chose to omit the Johannine writings, among others, from his own heretical canon of New Testament writings. Clearly he refused to accept the apostolic teaching of Holy Tradition. He refuted the Incarnation of the Son of God. He renounced the belief that being fully God the Lord emptied Himself and became fully man. He rejected the fact that the Son of God truly suffered in the flesh. And he repudiated the apostolic faith that Christ, as truly God, was crucified and truly died and was buried. Such

---

[106] 1 John 4. 2, 3.
[107] 2 John 7.

teachings, according to St. John the Theologian, could ultimately be of no other source than the Evil One himself—the Anti-Christ.

Certainly St. John is writing several decades before the appearance of Marcion. Still, his warning to Christian believers about rebellious false teachers who revolt against the apostolic teachings of Holy Tradition remain timeless and relevant for all ages: "Little children, it is the last hour; and as you have heard that the Antichrist is coming, even now many antichrists have come ... They went out from us, but they were not of us; for if they had been of us, they would have continued with us; but they went out that they might be made manifest, that none of them were of us."[108]

Another major feature that set Marcion apart from apostolic teaching was his rejection of the Old Testament. He saw a separation and contrast between the teachings of the Old Testament and those writings that would soon become our New Testament. Marcion believed that Christ came to *supplant* the Old Testament, not to fulfill it as our Lord Himself proclaimed.[109] According to Marcion, it was the God of the Law who prevailed in the Old Testament, and this Judaic understanding of reward or punishment for either keeping or breaking this Law was incompatible with what Marcion believed to be New Testament teaching. For Marcion, the New Testament Christ revealed not a God of Law, but the God of grace and love.[110]

---

[108] 1 John 2. 18, 19.
[109] See Matt. 5. 17.
[110] Cf. P. Chrestou, Ἑλληνικὴ Πατρολογία, vol. 2, p. 180.

Marcion therefore considered not only two 'testaments', but basically two different 'Gods' who were revealed in them. The Creator God of the Old Testament remained the God of Law, and there could be no relationship between this God and Jesus Christ who came to reveal the God of grace. The Old Testament was incompatible with the New Testament. This led Marcion to reject and deny the presence and manifestation of the pre-incarnate Son of God appearing in the various theophanies of the Old Testament.

However, for the Apostles and Holy Tradition as a whole, it is the *same* Person—the Son and Word of God (that is, the *pre*-Incarnate Son of God)—Who appeared to the Patriarchs, Prophets and Righteous in the Old Testament, Who is the *same* Person who was born of the Virgin Mary and became man as the Incarnate Word of God in the New Testament.[111]

Not only were Marcion's views of the Old Testament heretical, but his understanding of New Testament teachings also fell outside of Tradition. Marcion considered the majority of the Apostles to have been blinded by their Judaic roots of the Old Testament. This led him to reject much of what would become our New Testament writings. For Marcion, Christ ultimately had to call the Apostle Paul, since it was he alone of all the Apostles who finally came to comprehend the incompatibility between the God of Law of the Old Testament and the God of love of the New Testament.[112]

---

[111] See H. Boosalis, *Knowledge of God,* South Canaan, 2009, pp. 71-75.

[112] Cf. P. Chrestou, Ἑλληνικὴ Πατρολογία, vol. 2, p. 181.

Marcion not only rejected the entire Old Testament, but his New Testament canon contained only ten letters of the Apostle Paul and an edited version of the Gospel of Luke. As was mentioned earlier, this collection of New Testament writings, which Marcion created around the middle of the second century, is considered by some to be the first known canon of New Testament writings.[113]

Other ways in which Marcion contradicted Holy Tradition included his teaching on the complete avoidance of meat and wine as well as sexual relations, which were discouraged among his followers, since it led to the propagation of the human race. Those converts to his 'church' who were already married had to be divorced. Curiously, his 'church' could only be composed of converts, since marriage was forbidden. This is why many of his followers waited many years before actually converting, or else they simply remained catechumens.[114]

While he maintained the three degrees of ordination (bishop, priest and deacon) his clergy were more administrators than genuine recipients of a specially ordained grace. The offices of bishop, priest and deacon were periodically transferred back and forth from one person to another, even among unordained laymen. Of course, Marcion himself was the ultimate authority and hierarch of his heretical 'church'.[115]

---

[113] Cf. ibid.
[114] Cf. ibid., p. 184.
[115] Cf. ibid.

As strange as his teaching may appear to us today, this heresy of Marcion, which refused to accept the apostolic teachings of Holy Tradition, spread far and wide throughout the second century, from Rome and North Africa to Egypt, Syria, Greece and Asia Minor. His example is brought forward here to show how in the early Church many heretical currents flowed outside the boundaries of true apostolic teaching. And this highlights the very early significance of preserving this life of apostolic Tradition within the Orthodox Church.

Oral Tradition and Written Tradition

When discussing apostolic or Holy Tradition, it is customary to distinguish between oral tradition and written tradition.

St. Basil the Great, writing in the fourth century, provides a classic definition of the innate and organic relationship which unites these two traditions of the Church together as one, "Concerning the teachings of the Church ... we have received some from written sources, while others have been given to us secretly, through apostolic tradition. Both sources have equal force ..."[116]

This term 'secretly' is significant. In the original Greek it is 'ἐν μυστηρίῳ' which can mean in or through a "mystery" or "secret rite."[117] In the Orthodox Church, the term 'sacrament', although commonly accepted, is more accurately referred to as a 'mystery', coming from the direct translation of the Greek term 'τὸ μυστήριον', or in the plural 'τὰ μυστήρια'.[118] The term 'ἐν μυστηρίῳ' or 'secretly' as used in this context by St. Basil, may refer not only to oral teaching in general, but more specifically to the liturgical worship and sacramental rites of the Church.[119] The forms of these sacraments and other liturgical services were originally

---

[116] St. Basil the Great, *On the Holy Spirit* 27. 66, trans. D. Anderson, Crestwood, 1980, p. 98; PG 32, 188A.

[117] *A Patristic Greek Lexicon*, p. 891.

[118] Ibid, p. 892.

[119] Cf. J. Meyendorff, *Byzantine Theology*, p. 8.

passed down orally before finding their final written form. For St. Basil, many of the Church's teachings are thus preserved and transmitted not only through the writings of Holy Scripture, but in addition to, and more importantly, together *with* her liturgical and sacramental life.

In the context of explaining the Divine Liturgy and the Sacrament of Baptism in particular, St. Basil teaches:

If we attacked unwritten customs, claiming them to be of little importance, we would fatally mutilate the Gospel, no matter what our intentions—or rather, we would reduce the Gospel teachings to bare words. ... As everyone knows, we are not content in the liturgy simply to recite the words recorded by St. Paul or the Gospels, but we add other words both before and after, words of great importance for this mystery. We have received these words from unwritten teaching. ... What about baptizing a man with three immersions, or other baptismal rites, such as the renunciation of Satan and his angels? Are not all these things found in unpublished and unwritten teachings ...?[120]

---

[120] St. Basil the Great, ibid., pp. 98-99; PG 32, 188AC.

Writing even earlier than St. Basil, Tertullian (an ancient Christian writer from North Africa who lived from 160 to 220 AD) emphasized how it is only within the life of the Church wherein Holy Scripture is properly understood and interpreted. Tertullian argued that heretics should not even be allowed to use or discuss Holy Scripture, because it does not belong to them.[121] The natural place of Scripture is the Church. For only there can it be properly used and find the presuppositions for its correct and authentic interpretation.[122]

These examples are brought forward to show how in the early Church, Tradition was never considered as something that was added later to the Scriptures. Rather, Holy Tradition was seen as the *"milieu"* in which Scripture was properly understood.[123] There was never any question or debate over what took precedence over the other—Holy Tradition or Holy Scripture. They were never separated or somehow set in opposition to one another. The very existence of the New Testament presupposed the existence of the Church. The New Testament sprang up organically from within the life of the Church's Holy Tradition.

It is worth quoting a prominent Protestant theologian who correctly emphasizes how in the early Church there was never a need to deliberate over the proper relationship between Tradition and Scripture. There was no attempt to ascertain which had more authority, as if they were somehow against each other, as became the

---

[121] See Tertullian, *The Prescription Against Heretics* 15.
[122] See ibid., 21-22.
[123] J. Meyendorff, *Living Tradition*, p. 16.

case after the Reformation and still exists today. He also attests quite convincingly to the vital significance of Holy Tradition within the life of the early Church:

> In considering this question today, one must disregard modern considerations as to which had the greater significance, the written or the oral tradition. ... In the ancient church the really important thing was, first of all, that such a special concept as 'tradition' should even arise. [The] early Christian writers were convinced that the Christian religion includes certain propositions of faith and certain patterns of life, [and] that Christianity inherited both of these from the apostles, and that in the last analysis both of them go back to Jesus Christ ...[124]

One of the earliest writers to refer to this new and 'special concept' of Tradition is St. Irenaeus of Lyons (130-202). He appeals to the authority of Holy Tradition in the context of his refutation of Gnosticism, another early heresy which threatened the nascent Church. Much like the heresy of Marcion, and also the numerous heretical 'Christian' groups of our own day, the Gnostics too could quote extensively from Holy Scripture. They were often quite clever at it as well.

---

[124] B. Lohse, *A Short History of Christian Doctrine*, pp. 30-31.

Some scholars consider that the first scriptural commentaries written on the New Testament writings came not from within the Church but from certain Gnostic groups who tried to interpret these apostolic writings in light of their own heresy.[125] But because these heretical groups cut themselves off from the Church, and separated themselves from the life of Holy Tradition, they divorced themselves from the apostolic experience of the life in Christ. They were thus unable to correctly interpret and expound on the Scriptures of the apostolic Church.

It wasn't enough for the early Church to formally declare her own canon of New Testament writings and simply quote from her Holy Scripture. If she was to defend her teachings based on her apostolic experience of life in Christ, she needed to establish her Scriptural exegesis on the concrete practices and teachings which were lived out through her life of Holy Tradition. This proper interpretation of Holy Scripture can only be found within the life of the Church herself.

It was this 'new' phenomenon of Holy Tradition to which St. Irenaeus appealed to in his refutation of Gnosticism. He was convinced that the power of Holy Tradition united the true apostolic Church throughout the world, even among barbarian groups who managed to maintain this tradition without any formal written texts.[126]

---

[125] Eg., ibid., p. 32.

[126] Cf. St. Irenaeus, *Against Heresies* 3. 4. 2; PG7, 855C.

Among all the various peoples and nations—even those who did not share the same language—the Faith of the Apostles remained identical and its integrity preserved intact. St. Irenaeus explains:

> The Church ... though disseminated throughout the world, even to the ends of the earth, received from the apostles and their disciples the faith. ... The Church ... carefully guards this preaching and this faith which she has received, as if she dwelt in one house. She likewise believes these things as if she had but one soul and one and the same heart; she preaches, teaches, and hands them down harmoniously, as if she possessed but one mouth. For, although the languages throughout the world are dissimilar, nevertheless the meaning of the tradition is one and the same.[127]

The early Fathers protected the fullness of their apostolic experience through their appeal to Tradition. They never proclaimed Tradition as being superior to Scripture, as if they could contradict one another. Rather, there is a symbiotic relationship between the two. They give life to each other. They are mutually inclusive and intertwined. Each presupposes the other. Both enable the other's proper interpretation.[128]

---

[127] Ibid., 1. 10. 1-2, trans. D. Unger, New York, 1992, pp. 48-49; PG7, 549A-552B.

[128] Cf. C. Scouteris, Ἱστορία Δογμάτων, vol. 1, p. 494.

'Consensus Patrum', Liturgical Life and Sacred Hymnology

It is true that some bishops and Church Fathers may have had their own individual interpretations of Scripture, with particular theological opinions of their own. Such isolated teachings that fall outside the more commonly accepted patristic consensus are referred to as 'theologoumena' or private opinions.

It is amazing, however, when one considers the enormous amount of their writings, how by far the vast majority of patristic teachings are all in alignment and agreement with one another. Thus, the Church's authoritative interpretation or exegesis of Scripture, together with her official theological doctrines, became based on this commonly accepted consensus of patristic teachings. There arose an obvious and organic standard among the teachings of the Church Fathers—a 'consensus patrum'. It is these teachings which became the authoritative criterion on which later patristic writings were based, especially when, according to Meyendorff, they were "sanctified by liturgical and hymnographical usage."[129]

The Orthodox Church is indeed characterized by the abundance of her sacred hymnography. This hymnography is innate to the very life of the Church itself. These hymns and services, the structure and format of which are called the 'typica', comprise the complete

---

[129] J. Meyendorff, *Byzantine Theology*, p. 21.

expression of her liturgical life, including her yearly, weekly, daily and also paschal cycles of services: "This wealth of expression cannot be found elsewhere in the Christian world. ... Translated into the various vernacular languages of the Byzantine world—Slavic, Georgian, Arabic, and dozens of others—the liturgy was also a powerful expression of unity in faith and sacramental life."[130]

It is this multifaceted liturgical life, with its depth of sacred hymnography, which unites all Orthodox faithful into one organic body. This is where we find our Orthodox identity. This is where we live our common ecclesial life in Christ. This is why our personal participation in the sacramental and liturgical life of the Church is so vital to our overall spiritual lives as Orthodox Christians. Outside of this liturgical life, the ecclesial experience is incomplete.

This relates directly to the pastoral ministry of the parish priest. Among the various facets of his priestly ministry, his role as liturgical celebrant is fundamental. Together with his own personal pursuit of purification of passions and progress in prayer, his liturgical and sacramental functions provide a primary foundation which establishes, shapes and informs his teaching, preaching and pastoral ministries as well.

This unique liturgical life forms a constant and continuous expression of the inherent unity that bonds believers today with all the saints, Church Fathers and faithful from throughout the centuries. It bonds us not

---

[130] Ibid., p. 8.

only liturgically and sacramentally, but through our hymnography we sing out—as with one voice—the same shared theological teachings that unite all Orthodox into the One, Holy, Catholic and Apostolic Church.

Many if not all of our liturgical hymns and prayers, as well as the other elements of our sacramental rites and services, were composed by Church Fathers and saints. It was only natural for them to proclaim the commonly accepted patristic teachings in their own sacred hymns and prayers, especially when such teachings were officially declared as dogma by conciliar decree. The Church's dogmatic teachings are thus expressed not only through conciliar formulations, but through worship in our liturgical experience. Our sacred hymnology therefore serves as an invaluable expression of Orthodox theological doctrine.

The Role of Ethnic Customs

The life of Holy Tradition is experiential in nature. Tradition comes alive only when it is *given* life through one's free will; when it is incarnated in human persons—and human cultures—through the synergy of man's freedom and God's grace.

Not only does Holy Tradition come alive, but it vivifies those who earnestly pursue it and participate in it. This life of Holy Tradition is dynamic. Its content does not change. This remains eternal. However, its outward expression is open to a variety of ethnic expressions.

Holy Tradition thrives in whatever cultural context the Church may find herself. In this way, Holy Tradition transports the believer not so much to the Church's glorious *past*, but to the glory of her *eternal life*: "Through Tradition the Church is preserved alive and changeless ... and only through Tradition does the life of the Church arrive at each given moment in time. ... Tradition assures us of the eternity, inter-temporality and universality of the Gospel, which is lived within the Church at each and every historical present. ... Tradition is not simply the voice of the past; it is rather the voice of eternity."[131]

---

[131] C. Scouteris, 'Paradosis: The Orthodox Understanding of Tradition', p. 133.

The life of Holy Tradition surpasses the limits of local, ethnic or national customs. Yet by necessity it still must become embodied and embedded within a specific cultural community. In this way every ethnic group has elements that can uniquely contribute to this one identical yet limitless life in Christ.

Although it remains the same, Holy Tradition is expressed and experienced through a variety of languages and cultures. While there are many distinct parts that make up the one whole Body, with various expressions that manifest the one true Faith, the common life of Holy Tradition continuously binds us all as one Body.

All nations are called to this glorious Body of Christ. And every language has the potential to become a 'liturgical' language through which Christ is to be glorified and 'rightly worshiped'. Just as every nation, and even every tribe, has the natural right to read Holy Scripture in their own native language, so too should they have the same privilege to worship God in their own indigenous tongue.

And not only their native language, but also their native culture is open to this sacred transfiguration. Every culture has some basic features that can be consecrated in the light of Christ. This in turn not only transforms that particular culture, but it further enriches the living expression of Holy Tradition.

Before proceeding any further, it would be helpful to clarify the limits of this term 'culture'. Perhaps the term is too vague to even use. It can be so broad that it becomes cumbersome. In many cases 'culture' encompasses the entire ethos of a people or a nation.

This includes not only language and ethnic customs, but also religious beliefs and social norms, even music, art and dance, among others. Obviously, not all aspects of a given culture are open to adaptation in Christ. A more appropriate term for our context might be 'specific ethnic customs' or 'particular local traditions'.

This brings us back to the original question of our new, first-year seminarian. Is everything that we do in the Church a bona-fide part of Holy Tradition? Are all of the various local traditions essential components of our life in Christ? Are all those ethnic or local customs an integral part and direct expression of the life of the Holy Spirit in the Church? Do they all echo the 'voice of eternity' or are they more confined to a specific 'historical present' with little or no essential and eternal value?

Do some of our ethnic customs and local traditions actually detract from our unity and lead to a mutual estrangement among the faithful? Certainly most of these practices are not wrong or necessarily bad in themselves—but can they be? Can they be misconstrued to be something they are not? Can they tend to separate us from one another, making some of us more insular and isolated than we ought to be?

There are so many various components that make up the life of Holy Tradition. These include, but are not limited to: Holy Scripture, liturgical services, sacramental rites, dogmatic teachings, patristic writings, canon law, lives of saints, Church architecture, iconography and hymnology, to name but a few. All these elements form an organic whole and they cannot be dissected and effectively examined apart from one another.

Still we must ask the question: Which of these elements are more open to being adapted within a particular cultural context, and which are not? Certainly some are not up for discussion as to their viability. While Holy Scripture, liturgical services, dogmatic teachings and patristic writings must be translated into the various vernacular languages, their actual wording or essential content must not be changed in order to fit in to a specific culture.

On the other hand, Church architecture, iconography and music may indeed take on a variety of external forms, depending on particular ethnic customs. Such elements are obviously more open to cultural influence and may be adapted over time. We only have to look at the variety of our Church domes as an example. The symbolism remains the same, but the external expression is open to adaptation. Often this is positive. Sometimes it is not.

Another good example is Orthodox iconography. There are a variety of distinct schools from different countries and periods of history, up to and including our own day. We have all been touched by inspired iconography, which can convey the very spirit of Holy Tradition. But on the other hand, some of us have also seen some bad or even distasteful 'iconography', which may be overtly-influenced by western art and individual taste rather than the catholic life of Holy Tradition. The same could be said of our hymnology.

The point is that an 'artificial introduction' of any cultural influence often ends either in an outright rejection or a strained 'acceptance'. With the passing of time, such influences can have an opposite effect and lead to rigid conservatism and zealous fundamentalism. This is why Orthodox Christians today must learn to distinguish between that which is clearly common to our life of Holy Tradition—which is the life of the Holy Spirit guiding the Church—and that which is secondary or temporary and relates more to the practice of particular local and ethnic customs.

If we truly want to comprehend the unique quality of our shared ecclesial life of Holy Tradition we must first distinguish between that which is of permanent value and that which is secondary and in fact allows for the natural variety of our shared life.[132] This is especially crucial for those of us in the United States, where one senses a growing need for more of a 'Pan-Orthodox' outlook. This relates to not only how we see ourselves as 'Orthodox-Americans', but also how we see each other, that is to say, how we relate to and work with our fellow Orthodox faithful within the United States, on both national and local levels.

We must first learn to distinguish between the life of Holy Tradition and the practices of our ethnic customs that sometimes overshadow it. Only in this way will we maintain the integrity of Tradition as a whole. For once we elevate our ethnic forms to a position of 'artificial prestige' they then become something they were never meant to be. The very life of Holy Tradition

---

[132] Cf. J. Meyendorff, *Living Tradition*, pp. 21-22.

then becomes "petrified into the forms of a particular culture [which] not only excludes the others and betrays the catholicity of the Church, but it also identifies itself with a passing and relative reality and is in danger of disappearing with it."[133]

Let us continuously keep in mind, that as Orthodox believers especially in America today, we cannot close ourselves off completely from the society and culture in which we live. Yet at the same time we should not adopt just any element which someone might have a liking for. Perhaps there will always be such tension. Certain customs and local traditions will always try to be what they are not. Other customs will be embraced and new 'traditions' forged. Other local practices often eventually just fade away. Such is the cycle of life.

In conclusion, it is amazing to consider the dynamic and vibrant nature of the life of Holy Tradition. How is it that we Orthodox appear on the one hand so fanatically devoted to our cherished traditions, which often seem archaic and outdated, yet on the other hand we see ourselves as not bound but truly free?

The Church enjoys great liberty in expressing her ecclesial life in Christ. She is free to adopt whatever she chooses from the vast variety of ethnic customs of any culture wherein she may find herself. This is a paradox. It manifests our genuine freedom in Christ: "Now the Lord is Spirit; and where the Spirit of the Lord is, there is liberty."[134]

---

[133] Ibid., p. 26.
[134] 2 Cor. 3. 17.

I close with the following words from Fr. George Florovsky who writes:

> 'Tradition' … is a continuity of the abiding presence of the Holy Spirit in the Church, a continuity of divine guidance and illumination. The church is not bound by the 'letter'. Rather, she is constantly moved forth by the 'spirit'. The same spirit, the spirit of truth, which 'spake through the prophets', which guided the apostles, is still continuously guiding the church into the fuller comprehension and understanding of the divine truth, from glory to glory.[135]

May the same Holy Spirit who enlightened the Apostles at Pentecost continue to guide us now, as the Church moves forward, by God's grace, further into the twenty-first century.

---

[135] G. Florovsky, *Bible, Church, Tradition: An Eastern Orthodox View*, p. 106.

Epilogue: Holy Tradition Tomorrow

Today among the various Orthodox jurisdictions in the United States, many parishes are evolving into a new type of demographic. These parishes are basically an amalgamation of members from not only one particular ethnic jurisdiction, but rather a unique mixture consisting of a growing number of American converts, together with members from other Orthodox ethnic backgrounds as well.

On the one hand, we see that such parishes are indeed slowly becoming more 'Pan-Orthodox' in ethos and outlook. Various ethnic and local customs are being shared and adapted within a particular parish. This blending together is happening organically on its own, without any outside intervention. This trend will likely continue in the future.

But if the adaptation of any local or ethnic custom is to enjoy any whole-hearted acceptance among the faithful, there must exist an already innate affinity between any specific local tradition and the life of Holy Tradition as a whole. If it is to be genuinely received, it must not be forged or imposed artificially. Rather it should well up innately and naturally on its own, with its acceptance easy to embrace. Certain ethnic elements or local customs are obviously going to be more compatible than others, and thus more readily recognized as authentic expressions of our ecclesial life.

Ultimately it is up to a synod of bishops to make the final and authoritative decision. And not only our local synod of bishops within a particular jurisdiction, but now in America on a national level we have our Assembly of Bishops (The Assembly of Canonical Orthodox Bishops of North and Central America). It is they who will have the ultimate responsibility.

But the laity also have a formative impact. Rather than originating from the hierarchy and then being passed down, often times these adaptations begin organically among the people. Some practices become acceptable, others do not. And even if some new local tradition arises within a particular parish or diocese, it is nevertheless still up to the hierarchy to recognize and confirm it, or declare it as unacceptable.[136]

Yet on the other hand, we also have many other parishes which wish to remain anchored in their own ethnic identity. Such parishes also offer their own positive contribution to Orthodoxy in America. They provide a significant role with direct links to their mother countries as well as the perpetuation of their ethnic languages and customs, which are all very important to preserve.

If we are ever to attain any genuine level of Pan-Orthodox unity among the various ethnic jurisdictions here in the United States, to whatever degree, both types of parishes are needed. Both will make their own

---

[136] Interestingly, if any new adaptation or practice were to originate from the hierarchy, for whatever reason, then conversely it would ultimately be up to the entire *laos* to recognize and confirm it, collectively as the Body of Christ—and this includes the laity.

unique contributions. How this will happen has yet to be seen.

Still, any true sense of Pan-Orthodox unity remains far off into the future. Our new Assembly of Bishops is an encouraging sign. Nevertheless, any viable administrative unity in America is something that many of us may not see in our own lifetime.

However, there is something we can do right now. Rather than simply talking about a hypothetical 'Pan-Orthodox unity', let us begin by putting into practice something a bit more concrete. How about just a little more—'*inter-jurisdictional cooperation*'?

Select Bibliography

Patristic Writings

ATHANASIUS THE GREAT. *On the Incarnation.* Trans. C. S. M. V. Crestwood: St. Vladimir's Seminary Press, 1953.

BASIL THE GREAT. *On the Holy Spirit.* Trans. D. Anderson. Crestwood: St. Vladimir's Seminary Press, 1980.

—— *Hexaemeron.* Trans. B. Jackson. The Nicene and Post-Nicene Fathers, 2nd series, vol. 8. Grand Rapids: W. B. Eerdmans, 1989.

DIONYSIUS THE AREOPAGITE. *On the Divine Names.* Trans. P. Rorem. The Classics of Western Spirituality. New York: Paulist Press, 1987.

EUSEBIUS. *Ecclesiastical History.* Trans. G. A. Williamson. London: Penguin Books, 1965.

IRENAEUS OF LYONS. *Against the Heresies.* Trans. A. Roberts and J. Donaldson. The Ante-Nicene Fathers, vol. 1. Peabody: Hendrickson Publishers, 2004.

—— *On the Apostolic Preaching.* Trans. J. Behr. Crestwood: St. Vladimir's Seminary Press, 1997.

JOHN DAMASCENE. *Exact Exposition of the Orthodox Faith.* Trans. F. Chase. The Fathers of the Church, vol. 37. Washington, D.C.: The Catholic University of America Press, 1958.

—— *On the Divine Images.* Trans. D. Anderson. Crestwood: St. Vladimir's Seminary Press, 1980.

NICHOLAS CABASILAS. *The Life in Christ.* Trans. C. J. deCatanzaro. Crestwood: St. Vladimir's Seminary Press, 1974.

—— *Commentary on the Divine Liturgy.* Trans. J. M. Hussey and P. A. McNulty. Crestwood: St. Vladimir's Seminary Press, 1977.

TERTULLIAN. *Prescription Against Heretics.* Trans. P. Holmes. The Ante-Nicene Fathers, vol. 3. Peabody: Hendrickson Publishers, 2004.

Modern Authors

AMILIANOS, ARCHIMANDRITE. *The Way of the Spirit.* Trans. M. Maximos, Athens: Indiktos, 2009.

BOOSALIS, HARRY. *Knowledge of God.* South Canaan: St. Tikhon's Seminary Press, 2009.

CHRESTOU, PANAYIOTIS. *Ἑλληνική Πατρολογία*, vol. 2. Thessaloniki: Kyromanos, 1978.

CHRYSSAVGIS, JOHN. 'The Liturgy as Tradition and Tradition as Liturgy', *Sobornost* 7. 2, 1985.

—— *The Way of the Fathers.* Thessaloniki: Patriarchal Institute for Patristic Studies, 1998.

FLOROVSKY, GEORGES. *Aspects of Church History.* Vaduz: Buchervert., 1987.

—— *Bible, Church and Tradition: An Eastern Orthodox View.* Vaduz: Buchervert., 1987.

—— *Creation and Redemption.* Belmont: Nordland Publishing, 1976.

—— *The Ways of Russian Theology*, vols. 1 and 2. Belmont: Nordland Publishing, 1979 and 1987.

HIEROTHEOS, METROPOLITAN. *The Feasts of the Lord.* Trans. E. Williams. Levadia: Birth of the Theotokos Monastery, 2003.

―――― *The Mind of the Orthodox Church.* Trans. E. Williams. Levadia: Birth of the Theotokos Monastery, 1998.

LOSSKY, VLADIMIR. *In the Image and Likeness of God.* Crestwood: St. Vladimir's Seminary Press, 1985.

―――― *The Mystical Theology of the Eastern Church.* Crestwood: St. Vladimir's Seminary Press, 1976.

MANTZARIDIS, GEORGIOS. *Orthodox Spiritual Life.* Trans. K. Schram. Brookline: Holy Cross Press, 1994.

―――― *The Deification of Man.* Trans. L. Sherrard. Crestwood: St. Vladimir's Seminary Press, 1984.

―――― *Time and Man.* Trans. J. Vulliamy. South Canaan: St. Tikhon's Seminary Press, 1996.

MATSOUKAS, NIKOS. *Δογματικὴ καὶ Συμβολικὴ Θεολογία*, vol. 1. Thessaloniki: Pournaras, 1990.

MEYENDORFF, JOHN. *Byzantine Theology.* New York: Fordham University, 1974.

―――― *Living Tradition.* Crestwood: St. Vladimir's Seminary Press, 1978.

―――― *Catholicity and the Church.* Crestwood: St. Vladimir's Seminary Press, 1983.

POPOVICH, JUSTIN. *Orthodox Faith and Life in Christ.* Trans. A. Gerostergios. Belmont: Institute for Byzantine and Modern Greek Studies, 1994.

PORPHYRIOS, ELDER. *Wounded by Love.* Trans. J. Raffin. Evia: Holy Convent of the Life-giving Spring, Greece, 2005.

ROMANIDES, JOHN. *Δογματικὴ καὶ Συμβολικὴ Θεολογία τῆς Ὀρθοδόξου Καθολικῆς Ἐκκλησίας,* vol. 1. Thessaloniki: Pournaras, 2004.

—— *Patristic Theology.* Trans. Hieromonk Alexios (Trader). The Dalles: Uncut Mountain Press, 2008.

—— *An Outline of Orthodox Patristic Dogmatics.* Trans. G. D. Dragas, Rollinsford: Orthodox Research Institute, 2004.

SCOUTERIS, CONSTANTINE. *Ἱστορία Δογμάτων,* vol. 1. Athens: Diegesis Publishers, 1998.

—— 'Paradosis: The Orthodox Understanding of Tradition' in *Ecclesial Being,* ed. C. Veniamin, South Canaan: Mount Thabor Publishing, 2005.

SOPHRONY, ARCHIMANDRITE. *Saint Silouan the Athonite.* Trans. R. Edmonds. Essex: Stavropegic Monastery of St. John the Baptist, 1991.

STANILOAE, DUMITRU. 'The Orthodox Conception of Tradition and the Development of Doctrine', *Sobornost* 5. 9, 1969.

STYLIANOPOULOS, THEODORE. *The New Testament: An Orthodox Perspective.* Brookline: Holy Cross Press, 1997.

VASILEIOS, ARCHIMANDRITE. *Hymn of Entry.* Trans. E. Brière (Theokritoff). Crestwood: St. Vladimir's Seminary Press, 1984.

———— Ἀπολυτίκιον. Karyes: Holy Monastery of Iveron, 2011.

———— 'Everything is Prayer', *The Orthodox Word* 279, 2011.